FIFTY WAYS TO TEACH WITH TECHNOLOGY

TIPS FOR ESL / EFL TEACHERS

PAUL RAINE

WAYZGOOSE PRESS

Fifty Ways to Teach with Technology: Tips for ESL/EFL Teachers

Copyright © 2018 by Paul Raine

Cover design by DJ Rogers.

Edited by Dorothy Zemach.

Published in the United States by Wayzgoose Press.

CONTENTS

HOW TO USE THIS BOOK

Most teachers use a textbook in class, which provides both instruction and practice – but, often, not enough practice. Students need to practice again and again, and in different ways, not just to keep their interest but to both learn and remember.

This book gives you ideas to help your students with their study of English through the use of technology. It can be used with any textbook, or without any textbook at all. Some of the ideas can be used in class, and some out of class or for independent student projects.

Not every idea will work for every student or for every class. That's why there are fifty. We feel sure that many of the ideas presented here will bring you results if you try them sincerely and practice them regularly.

Here is a suggested method for using this book:

1) Read through all of the fifty tips without stopping.

2) Read through the tips again. Choose five or six that you think might work for your class. Decide when you will try them.

3) Choose different types of ideas: some that can be done independently, and some that work along with your textbook.

4) Each time you use one of the ways, make a note about how well it worked for your class and why. Remember that most of the tips will work best if you use them several times (or even make them a habit). Don't try a tip only once and decide it's no good for your students. Give the tips you try a few chances, at least.

5) Every few weeks, read through the tips again, and choose some new ones. Discontinue using any methods that are not working for you.

Finally, consider trying some of the other books in our *50 Ways to Teach* series. No one skill in English is really separate from the others. Speaking, listening, reading, writing, vocabulary, and grammar are all connected. Students who improve in one area will almost always improve in other areas too.

INTRODUCTION

Most teachers have used technology of some kind in their classrooms. Many are interested in learning more about how best to utilize the wide range of technological devices now available to educators, from laptops to smartphones, from IC recorders to video cameras, from desktop software to cloud-based services.

This book provides ideas to help you and your students leverage technology for the best language learning outcomes. Whether you wish to use students' own mobile devices, conduct an effective and engaging lesson in a CALL lab, or simply expand your list of language learning websites, this book has a wide selection of ideas for you.

Not every student has a smartphone, and not every institution has a computer lab. That's why the 50 ideas in this publication cover a wide range of software and hardware that can be used in a variety of learning and teaching contexts. Seasoned technophiles and apprehensive technophobes alike will find this list of ideas and activities of value.

Before you begin trying out the ideas in this book, here are some general points of advice about successfully using technology in the classroom, and how to overcome problems if they do arise.

1. Be prepared to give technical support to your students. Computer literacy varies immensely within classes that may otherwise be streamed for language ability. While some students may be competent at tweeting, Googling, and running their own blogs, others may struggle with simple tasks such as copy and paste. Take it slow, and go at the pace of the least confident learner. Try out websites and applications yourself before class (especially if you have not used them recently) to remind yourself of what students will encounter when using them for the first time.

2. Many websites require registration, especially to access more advanced features such as tracking progress. Have students write down their login details in a safe place, or use the same login details that they use for their university or school account. Otherwise, be prepared for students constantly forgetting their login credentials!

3. Ensure you have a reliable power supply and that devices you want to use are fully charged before starting your class. Don't forget to bring all the appropriate power adapters for your computers,

video camera, etc. If you are having students use their own devices, let them use your institution's power outlets to recharge if necessary.

4. Check that everything is working before you begin the lesson. Have a backup activity planned for when things go wrong. Sudden power cuts or network outages can derail even the best-planned lessons. Also, remind students of the golden rule: save your work regularly!

5. Unplug occasionally. Make sure students spend some time away from the screen, and take regular breaks during longer sessions. Have a couple of lo-tech activities planned in addition to your hi-tech tasks.

PART I

AUDIO & VIDEO

LISTENING TO AUDIO RECORDINGS

Introduction

The widespread use of recorded audio for language learning has been around since the language learning labs of the 1960s and 70s (Schwartz, 1995), with listening being given particular prominence in the Audio-Lingual Method (ALM) (Nagaraj, 2003).

Although ALM itself is now obsolete, recorded audio retains a major role in language learning classrooms. The most apparent benefit of recorded audio is the ability to expose learners to a variety of different speakers without them actually having to travel to a place where the target language is being used (Arshavskaya, 2018). Recorded audio also gives teachers and learners much greater control over the spoken content, including the ability to pause, rewind, and even slow down speech (East & King, 2012).

Some experts argue that listening alone is sufficient to gain a very high level of competence in a second language (e.g. Saville-Troike, 2006) and others note that it is a necessary prerequisite for speaking (Krashen & Terrell, 1983; Nunan, 1997). Whatever your beliefs about the theoretical importance of listening, it is clear that recorded audio opens the door to an abundance of language learning activities.

Resources

Hardware

- Smartphone or tablet (iOS/Android)
- Desktop or laptop (Windows/Mac OS)

Websites

- ELLLO: http://www.elllo.org
- VOA News: http://learningenglish.voanews.com
- Storyline: https://www.storylineonline.net
- BBC Learning English: http://www.bbc.co.uk/learningenglish
- ESL Lab: https://www.esl-lab.com
- Lyrics Training: https://lyricstraining.com
- English Listening: https://www.englishlistening.com

————

1. English Listening Lesson Library Online (ELLLO): The Internet provides a wealth of recorded audio and listening comprehension activities for learners of English. These can be studied independently by students or used by teachers to supplement their textbook.

One of the biggest repositories of free listening activities is the English Listening Library Online, which also offers a range of listening comprehension activities and transcriptions of audio recordings.

———

2. Lyrics Training: Another innovative online listening tool is provided by Lyrics Training. This website allows learners to enjoy their favorite songs while also practicing their listening comprehension skills by completing real-time cloze (fill-in-the-blank) activities with the selected song's lyrics.

MAKING AUDIO RECORDINGS

Introduction

From cassette tapes in the 70s and 80s, to MiniDiscs and Compact Disks in the 90s, to digital audio recorders at the turn of the millennium, and finally to tablet and smartphone based recording apps in the 21st century: the facility to easily record audio for pedagogical purposes has been available for at least 50 years.

Recording audio allows teachers to obtain evidence of student oral output for grading or feedback purposes (Harmer, 2004). Students may also wish to use their own device to record classroom proceedings for later review of linguistic structure and content, as well as an aid to speech perception (Saville-Troike, 2006).

Students can also make audio recordings for self-reflective purposes, or to identify and correct their own errors and those of their classmates (Hedge, 2008).

Resources

Hardware

- Smartphone or tablet (iOS/Android)
- Desktop or laptop (Windows/Mac OS) with mic
- IC recorder

Software

- Toau: for Mac OS: http://25.io/toau
- Voice Memos: iOS
- Hi-Q MP3: Android

Websites

- Voice Thread: http://www.voicethread.com

———

3. Repeated self-transcription: Choose a simple topic (such as "A mistake I made" or "A time I felt angry") and have students brainstorm bullet-points for their spoken answer. Remind them that they should not be writing in full sentences at this stage. Next, give students one minute to speak and record their answers using an IC recorder or smartphone.

Very short, spoken monologues such as this are good practice for standardized tests such as the TOEFL iBT.

Students listen to and transcribe their own spoken answers, without correcting any mistakes. Students then check the word count in their transcription, circle any mistakes, and make improvements. Repeat the activity with the same topic, and let students see their improvement from their first attempt.

———

4. Voice Thread: Voice Thread is an innovative and intuitive website that allows you to easily create a conversation with your students. It offers a "multi-sensory" environment that supports audio, video, images, and documents. It allows users to comment on uploaded media via microphone, webcam, text, phone, and audio-file upload. It can also be integrated into a variety of Learner Management Systems (LMS).

WATCHING VIDEO RECORDINGS

Introduction

Video made its way into language classrooms with the advent of VHS in the late 1970s, and video-based courses such as the BBC's *Follow Me* (Goldstein, 2014). The use of video was given a boost by the popularity of the Communicative Language Approach (CLT), and interactive tasks were generated by teacher manipulation of audio, video, and subtitle tracks (Goldstein, 2014).

CLT also emphasized the importance of using "authentic" materials in the classroom, and video was no exception. Authentic videos are said to present "real" language meant for native speakers (Stempleski, 1992). They provide 'slices of living language', with the level of encoded realism greater than that of text or audio based media (Allan, 1985).

Non-authentic videos, on the other hand, such as the well-known *Family Album USA* (Kelty, Cooperman, & Lefferts, 1991) tend to feature graded language, and a slower than average speed of speech. They often focus on educating the viewer about aspects of the target culture, such as life in America.

Resources

Hardware

- Smartphone or tablet (iOS/Android)
- Desktop or laptop (Windows/Mac OS)

Websites

- TED: http://www.ted.com/talks
- YouTube: http://www.youtube.com
- EngVid: http://www.engvid.com
- Film English: http://www.film-english.com
- Real English: http://www.real-english.com
- ESL Video: https://www.eslvideo.com
- Ed Puzzle: https://edpuzzle.com
- Tube Quizard: http://tubequizard.com
- Udemy: http://www.udemy.com

———

5. TED Talk paper: This activity works particularly well for TED talks (http://www.ted.com/talks), but can also be adapted for other types of video.

First, students choose a talk that appeals to them. After watching the talk (both with and without subtitles), they begin the writing process. In the first paragraph they introduce the talk and explain why they chose it. Following this, they write a short summary of the content of the talk. Next, they expand on the content of the talk by referencing external materials, such as websites and books. Then, they describe their reaction to the talk, and relate its contents to their own lives. Finally, they provide a conclusion and a list of references.

———

6. What happens next? This is a good activity to get students predicting likely outcomes of actions, and expressing degrees of certainty. It also helps them improve their ability to describe visual information. Prepare the activity by finding a selection of videos on YouTube with unexpected or unusual outcomes.

Show the first video and pause it before the unexpected action occurs. Have students answer these questions:

- Where is the video set?
- Who is in the video?
- What are they doing?
- What do you think will happen next?
- What would you do in the same situation and why?

Then show the remainder of the video and ask one final question:

- What actually happened?

This activity can be built upon for higher level classes by getting students to take on the teacher's role, find their own videos, and set the same questions to their partners.

————

7. Student subtitling and subtitle translation: This activity is suitable for high-level classes. First, prepare a selection of short video clips; movie trailers and English language commercials work well for this purpose. Upload all of the videos to your YouTube account.

Ensure you turn on community contributions (http://support.google.com/youtube/answer/6052538) for your videos, which will allow your students to add subtitles and captions to them. Have students access YouTube and navigate to your videos. Students then watch the videos, and create L1 subtitles or L2 captions for the dialogue.

————

8. Film English: Film English is an award-winning blog with a wide selection of free video-based lessons. The videos cover a variety of topics and target language, and stream directly from Vimeo or YouTube for the teacher's convenience. Detailed lesson plans are provided for each of the videos, as well as ideas for additional and follow-up activities.

MAKING VIDEO RECORDINGS

Introduction

Video recording devices have been used in language classrooms since the availability of cassette-based consumer camcorders in the mid 1980s. These days, virtually every teacher and student has a 1080p HD video recorder integrated into their smartphone or tablet, with the transition to 4K well underway in most devices.

However, in language teaching it is often audio quality that is more highly valued than video quality. Unfortunately, smartphones and tablets often fall short of delivering audio of an acceptable quality, mainly due to underpowered onboard microphones. A good selection of external microphones are available for smartphones, including table top, shotgun, and lavaliere types. If you are doing a lot of work with video recording in the classroom, an investment in an external microphone would probably be worthwhile.

The benefits of video recording are similar to those of recording of audio: teachers can collect evidence of their students' oral skills, with the added bonus of preserving non-verbal information such as gesture, body language, posture, facial expression and eye-contact.

Giving students the opportunity to perform in front of video via role-play and improvisation can also help increase motivation and interest (Katchen, 1991; Forrest, 1992).

In addition, learner-generated video projects provide the chance for students to develop and demonstrate "turn-taking strategies" for daily conversation (Biegel, 1998), as well as being able to review and evaluate their own performances (Akdeniz, 2017).

Resources

Hardware

- Smartphone or tablet (iOS/Android)
- Desktop or laptop (Windows/Mac OS)
- Video camera with external mic

Software

- iMovie: http://www.apple.com/mac/imovie
- Final Cut Pro: http://www.apple.com/final-cut-pro
- Sony Vegas Pro: http://www.sonycreativesoftware.com/vegaspro

Websites

- Internet Movie Script Database: http://www.imsdb.com
- Movie Tools: http://www.movietools.info
- Binumi: https://www.binumi.com
- YouTube: http://www.youtube.com
- We Video: http://www.wevideo.com

———

Using Pre-Made Dialogues

9. Text-book dialogue performance: If your textbook contains role-play dialogues with model audio or video tracks, have students choose one, rehearse and memorize it, and then perform in front of the camera. Students can use their own camera phones, or the teacher can record performances with a more advanced camera.

———

10. Movie dialogue performance: Have students brainstorm their favorite (English language) movies, or provide a list of suggestions. Next, get students to choose their favorite scene from one of the movies, or provide a list of suggestions.

Check the scripts for the movies online (e.g. http://www.imsdb.com), or have students watch a subtitled version and copy the dialogue from the subtitles.

Students rehearse the dialogue until it is memorized, and then perform it in front of the class or a camera.

————

Developing Original Dialogues

11. Situation, Complication, Resolution: Have students brainstorm situations (e.g. an airport, a classroom, a theme park, etc.). Students then think of a "complication" that may arise in that situation (e.g. forgetting a passport, arriving late for class, losing a wallet) and a "resolution" to the complication, i.e. what happens in the end.

Next, students form small groups of three or four people. Each member of the group plays a character in the situation (e.g. airport staff, customer, security guard, etc.). Students then construct original dialogues for the situation. Students rehearse their dialogues and perform them in front of a video camera. The whole class can then view videos, and comprehension questions can be devised as a follow-up activity.

Using Special Equipment

12. Using a green screen: For more ambitious video productions, consider using a green screen to change the setting behind the students when they act out their dialogues. This not only provides a greater sense of realism (in the final video), it also allows for a greater range of settings without ever leaving the classroom. It also encourages students to stretch their imaginations when acting out the dialogues according to whatever setting will be displayed behind them.

Green screens can be purchased online from around US$20, depending on size. In order to change the background in post-production, you will need a video editor with a "chroma key" facility, such as iMovie or Final Cut Pro for the Mac or Sony Vegas Pro for Windows PCs.

PART II
WEB-BASED ACTIVITIES

CLOUD SERVICES

Introduction

According to Amazon, which popularized the term with the launch of their Elastic Cloud Compute service in 2006, Cloud Computing is "the on-demand delivery of compute power, database storage, applications, and other IT resources through a cloud services platform via the internet" (Amazon, 2018).

Also in 2006, Google announced Google Docs, which moved traditionally desktop-based word processing into the web browser. Incremental improvements and additions, including Spreadsheets and Slides, eventually lead to the 2012 launch of Google Drive, described as "a hybrid of cloud storage and cloud computing" (Magid, 2012).

For teachers and students the world over, this meant being able to collaborate instantly, access documents from any device, and never again having to worry about clicking the "save" button (although many are distressed by its absence!). Similar cloud services later became available from the likes of Apple and Microsoft, but Google has become the dominant player in the classroom (Singer, 2017).

Resources

Hardware

- Smartphone or tablet (iOS/Android)
- Desktop or laptop (Windows/Mac OS)
- Google Chromebook

Websites

- Google Drive: http://drive.google.com
- Apple iCloud: http://www.icloud.com
- Microsoft OneDrive: https://onedrive.live.com
- is.gd: http://is.gd

––––––

13. Real time peer correction: Before class, access Google Drive and create a new folder. Share the folder with all your students (copy and paste their email addresses into the "share" dialog box—note that to access the shared folder, students will need to sign up for a Google account if they don't already have one). Students will then need to access their email account and accept the invitation to the shared folder.

Have your students access the shared folder and create a new document, titled with their own name. Students then complete a short writing assignment within the document. Edits are saved automatically. When students have finished the first draft, instruct them to close their own document and open another document in the same folder (one of their classmates' documents).

Have students look for spelling or grammar mistakes, and make comments within the document, highlighting any mistakes they find. After they have found two or three mistakes, they open the next document.

Repeat the activity until each student has checked at least five of their classmates' documents. Students then return to their own document and correct the highlighted mistakes.

————

14. Collaborative vocabulary translation: Create a new spreadsheet in Google Drive. Share the document with all of your students, or create it in a folder that is already shared. Populate the first column of the spreadsheet with a list of words you wish your students to learn. Instruct students to access the document. Assign each student a row or a range of rows. Instruct them to enter the L1 equivalent for each word in the second column of the document.

Extension: Have students enter the part of speech to be

entered in the third column, an example sentence in the fourth column, etc.

When all words have been translated, import the data into a vocabulary learning tool to allow students to study the vocabulary in a variety of ways.

––––––

15. Self-grading quizzes: Create a new form in Google Drive. Create a selection of text-based or multiple choice questions within the form. Don't forget to include a space for students to enter identifying information, such as their names or student numbers. Click the "cog" button in the top right of the page, and then click the "Quizzes" tab. Check the toggle on for the option "Make this a quiz". Return to the form and make sure you input the correct answers for each question.

Provide your students with a link to the form (use an URL shortener such as http://is.gd for long links). Administer the quiz to your students without having to worry about marking the answers yourself!

LANGUAGE LEARNING SYSTEMS

Introduction

It is important to encourage students to continue their English studies independently outside of the classroom. However, it can be difficult for students to find ample opportunity to use and practice English, especially when learning English as a foreign language.

There are a number of comprehensive web and app based language study platforms available to students who wish to take their learning into their own hands.

Resources

Hardware

- Smartphone or tablet (iOS/Android)
- Desktop or laptop (Windows/Mac OS)

Websites

- Duolingo: http://www.duolingo.com
- Busuu: https://www.busuu.com
- Babbel: http://www.babbel.com
- Apps 4 EFL: http://www.apps4efl.com

––––––

Tip 16. Duolingo: Duolingo is one of the most popular free language learning platforms, with over 300 million users (Lardinois, 2018). Numerous independent studies (e.g. Vesselinov & Grego, 2012), have vouched for its effectiveness, and teachers can track the progress of students in their classes, as well as assign homework tasks.

––––––

Tip 17. Apps 4 EFL: The author of this book has developed a website for English language learners and teachers, featuring a variety of web-based tools and activities, including automatic cloze creation and inline translation, vocabulary learning flashcard games, text-to-speech listening practice, and speech recognition pronunciation practice, along with many other features.

Apps 4 EFL is completely free and compatible with both desktops and mobile devices. It also offers comprehensive student management and tracking features for teachers.

VIRTUAL WORLDS

Introduction

Neal Stephenson's seminal sci-fi novel *Snow Crash* popularized the idea of exploring a Virtual World (VW) as an "avatar" back in 1992, and since then the concept has become mainstream, with the massive popularity of titles such as Second Life (2003) and Minecraft (2011).

VWs are often delivered in the form of Massively Multiplayer Online Roleplay Games (MMORPGs), which allow users to interact with other players, explore and create immersive 3D environments, collaborate on missions, and "level up" their characters.

Studies on the use of VWs for language learning have highlighted the benefits of the conversational interactions and creative aspects they provide (Hislope, 2009), and note that users can develop their pragmatic, syntactic, semantic and discoursal knowledge by solving content based problems through intercultural collaboration (Zheng et al, 2009). VWs are also highly conducive to both situated and experiential learning.

Resources

Hardware

- Desktop or Laptop (Windows/Mac OS)

Software

- Minecraft: http://www.minecraft.net
- Second Life: http://www.secondlife.com
- Open Wonderland: http://openwonderland.org
- Active Worlds: https://www.activeworlds.com

———

18. Teach English in a virtual world: Virtual worlds allow students to interact in ways that are impossible in real life. Traditional teaching techniques such as Total Physical Response (TPR) can be given a new lease of life inside a virtual environment, such as those provided by Minecraft or Second Life. Entire language learning communities can be built up using virtual worlds.

WEB 2.0 ACTIVITIES

Introduction

When the Internet became widely accessible in the early 1990s, it was characterized by Web 1.0 technologies. Web pages were generally static, and collaboration between users was limited. However, as both server-side and client-side systems and software developed, the range of possibilities for online interaction and collaboration rapidly increased.

By the early 2000s, Web 2.0 features allowed for the development of photo sharing sites such as Flickr, openly editable encyclopedias such as Wikipedia, and a vast array of blogs powered by the likes of Blogger, WordPress, and others (O'Reilly, 2009).

Web 2.0 usage in education has been a general consequence of the proliferation of network connected devices amongst teachers and learners, and has become an "indispensable component" of academic life (Wang & Camilla, 2012), with over 80% the "Net Generation" (those born between the early 80s and early 90s) having Social Network Service (SNS) profiles (McBride, 2009).

In their meta-analysis of research in the area of Web 2.0 and language learning, Wang and Camilla (2009) found that students' writing skills were most likely to benefit from Web 2.0 interventions, with writing confidence and strategies improving for many study participants (Wang & Camilla, 2009).

Web 2.0 environments have also been shown to be "comfortable," "collaboration-oriented," and "community-based," with most learners having a positive view of Web 2.0 tools and activities (Wang & Camilla, 2009).

Resources

Hardware

- Smartphone or tablet (iOS/Android)
- Desktop or laptop (Windows/Mac OS)

Websites

- Facebook: http://www.facebook.com
- Band: https://band.us/en
- Padlet: http://www.padlet.com
- PhraseMix: http://www.phrasemix.com
- Easier English Wiki: http://eewiki.newint.org

- Simple English Wikipedia:
  http://simple.wikipedia.org
- WordPress: http://www.wordpress.com
- Blogger: http://www.blogger.com

―――――

19. Self-introduction activity with Padlet: Padlet functions as a virtual pin-board that can be simultaneously updated by multiple users. It supports text, images, videos, and a variety of other file types. It is compatible with both PCs and mobile devices.

You can use Padlet for an innovative self-introduction activity. First, create a new Padlet wall. Next, have each student access the wall, and create a post with a written self-introduction and a photo of themselves or something they like. The Padlet wall updates in real time, so students can immediately see updates made by their classmates. After all the self-introductions have been created, students read through them.

Next, ask questions about the information displayed, e.g. *Who has a dog called Pochi?* or *How often does Hamid play tennis?* Students find the answers by scanning through the information as quickly as possible.

After your demonstration, students can quiz their partner about other classmates in the same way.

―――――

20. Collaboration through virtual groups: Social Network Services (SNS) such as Facebook or Band can be used to create virtual groups for class members to share ideas, exchange information and data, ask questions about homework, etc. Students sometimes take the initiative and create groups by themselves, but it can be better to have an official class group that you create to ensure all members of the class are included. You can also post updates and announcements to the group yourself.

Groups are more convenient than mailing lists, and quicker and more lightweight than a fully featured LMS.

---

21. Shared listening journals: Blogs can be used for a variety of language learning purposes, most commonly writing and reading practice. However, you can also take advantage of the multimedia aspect of blogs by getting your students to create a shared listening journal.

First, sign up for a hosted blog with WordPress, Blogger, or another provider. Grant author access to each student you wish to contribute to the blog.

After the blog is set up, have students to go to YouTube and find English-language videos (music videos and movie trailers work well for this purpose). After watching the videos, students copy the URLs and embed the videos in a new blog post. They then choose at least three English words or phrases that appear in the videos and copy them into the blog post, along with their L1 translations.

Additional questions that can be answered include:

- Who is in this video?
- What is the movie or song about?
- Why did you choose this video?
- How do you feel when you watch this video?

As each new blog entry is posted, students watch and comment on the entries made by their classmates. This is also a good way to get an insight into the movie and music preferences of your class.

————

22. Blogs and wikis for English learners: There is a vast range of blogs and wikis available online catering to an almost infinite array of interests. While higher-level English learners can improve their English by reading blogs and wikis catering to native English speakers, lower to mid-level learners will struggle to understand them. Therefore it is better for such learners to access sites that specifically cater to them through graded language.

Recommendations of such sites are Phrase Mix, the Simple English Wikipedia, and the Easier English Wiki. These blogs and wikis can either be studied independently by students, or used as a supplement to in-class materials.

PART III

LEARNING MATERIALS

PRE-MADE LESSON PLANS

Introduction

There comes a day in every ESL teacher's life where you need pre-made materials, and you need them now! Fortunately, there is a multitude of websites offering pre-made materials for ESL. Most of them are free, although some require user registration and sometimes a small monthly fee.

Resources

Hardware

- Smartphone or tablet (iOS/Android)
- Desktop or laptop (Windows/Mac OS)

Websites

- Breaking News English: http://www.breakingnewsenglish.com
- Film English: http://www.film-english.com
- Internet TESL Journal: http://iteslj.org/questions
- English Tips: http://www.englishtips.org
- ESL Video: http://www.eslvideo.com
- English Club: http://www.englishclub.com
- One Stop English: http://www.onestopenglish.com
- ESL Library: http://www.esl-library.com
- Sparklebox: http://www.sparklebox.co.uk
- TEFL.net: http://www.tefl.net

———

23. Breaking News English: Breaking News English is one of many free websites developed and maintained by prolific online materials creator Sean Banville (http://breakingnewsenglish.com/banville.html).

It features up-to-date news-based lessons on a variety of stories suitable for English learners, and a multitude of activities for every text, including listening practice, vocabulary matching, true and false questions, gap fills, comprehension questions, multiple choice quizzes, role-plays, surveys, discussion questions and more!

Best of all, it's completely free and no login or registration is required to access over 2,600 lessons categorized into seven difficulty levels.

DIGITAL TEXTS

Introduction

The idea of the paperless office was first posited in the mid 1970s, but despite optimistic predictions that Personal Computers would eliminate the need to print documents or make copies, this vision of the future failed to materialize, with the average 21st century office worker using 10,000 sheets of copy paper every year (O'Mara, 2016).

The reality of a paperless classroom has also failed to come to pass, especially in educationally conservative countries such as Japan, where there is still a preference for paper over digital materials amid concerns about student access to compatible devices (Gardner, 2016).

Notwithstanding the fact that many educational institutions are far from going fully paperless, ebooks offer a range of significant advantages over "dead tree" alternatives, chief among them the possibility of including interactive tasks and multimedia elements such as video and audio.

There are a range of tools and techniques available to teachers wishing to create digital texts from scratch, or convert existing materials into digital forms.

Resources

Hardware

- Smartphone or tablet (iOS/Android)
- Desktop or laptop (Windows/Mac OS)

Software

- iBooks Author: http://www.apple.com/ibooks-author
- Adobe Acrobat Pro: http://www.adobe.com/products/acrobatpro.html
- Calibre: http://calibre-ebook.com

Websites

- Storybird: http://www.storybird.com
- Twine: http://www.twinery.org
- Interactive Fiction Database: http://ifdb.tads.org

———

24. Creating interactive textbooks with iBooks Author:
If your students all have access to an Apple device (iMac/iPad/iPhone), consider using iBooks Author to create multimedia-rich and interactive textbooks for your students. The software is free and provides a variety of widgets for interactivity, including a multiple-choice question review activity.

For more information on creating EFL publications with iBooks Author, check here:
http://sites.google.com/site/getstartedwithiba.

———

25. Creating interactive PDFs with Adobe Acrobat Pro:
To create more universally accessible textbooks and worksheets, consider using Adobe Acrobat Pro.

One of the most convenient features of Adobe Acrobat Pro is the form creation function, which allows you to convert existing paper-based worksheets into interactive digital worksheets.

To do this, first scan in your paper-based worksheet as a PDF. Next, open the PDF with Acrobat Pro and select the "create form" function. Acrobat Pro will automatically scan the document and insert text-boxes where it thinks answers should be written. Minor adjustments can be made manually.

Once the PDF is saved, it can be distributed to students and edited in Adobe Reader and other free PDF viewers.

----

26. Creating illustrated story books with Story Bird:
Story Bird is a free web-based app for creating illustrated story books, which can either be published and read online, or ordered and printed on physical media. Story Bird provides a wide selection of artwork that can be freely used to create picture books, poems, and even full-length novels.

If you register as a teacher, you can also create and manage classes of students.

----

27. Creating non-linear (multi-path) stories with Twine: There has been a recent resurgence in the popularity of non-linear or multi-path stories (e.g. http://atama-ii.com), both in general fiction and EFL.

Twine is a web-based and desktop (Mac/PC) app that allows users to easily create such stories with an intuitive graphical interface. Once stories have been created, they can be published to HTML and shared on any website.

A wide selection of non-linear stories can be found at the Interactive Fiction Database.

PRESENTATION TOOLS AND TECHNIQUES

Introduction

We have come a long way since 1801, when James Pillans hung a large piece of slate on the wall of his Edinburgh classroom and invented the blackboard.

Although "chalk and talk" is still a mainstay of many classrooms, more fortunate teachers now have access to a high definition projector or plasma screen, if not an interactive whiteboard.

Laptops, tablets, and even smartphones can have their displays "mirrored" on a large screen in order to share information with students, and a wide variety of software is available to make the process easy and intuitive.

Resources

Hardware

- Smartphone or tablet (iOS/Android)
- Desktop or laptop (Windows/Mac OS)
- Apple TV

Software

- Notability: iOS, http://www.gingerlabs.com
- GoodReader: iOS, http://www.goodreader.com
- Preview: Installed by default on Mac OS
- Adobe Reader: Mac OS/Windows/iOS/Android, http://get.adobe.com/reader

Websites

- Prezi: http://www.prezi.com
- PowToon: http://www.powtoon.com

———

28. Projecting PDF annotations: PDFs are the closest thing we have to universal, cross-platform digital texts that can be easily annotated with freely available software. Adobe Reader (Mac OS/Windows) lets you add text and diagrammatic annotations to PDFs, as does Preview on Mac OS. If you connect your PC to your projector, you can then easily share your annotations with your entire class.

If you want to annotate PDFs on an iPad, there are a couple of options available. Two of the best iOS apps for this purpose are GoodReader and Notability. Both offer a comprehensive set of annotation tools, as well as syncing and sharing facilities. You can connect your iPad to your projector wirelessly via Apple TV, or via a wired HDMI or VGA connection.

———

29. Teacher or student created digital presentations: Several tools exist for spicing up traditional slide-based presentations. Prezi provides a wide selection of themes, fonts, and transitions to make dynamic and interactive presentations. This is a good tool for self-introductory activities and a variety of other content.

After a student has created a presentation, it can be easily shared with classmates and used as a listening and reading comprehension activity.

PART IV

REFERENCE MATERIALS

DICTIONARIES AND LINGUISTIC DATABASES

Introduction

Dictionaries have come a long way since the 1755 publication of Robert Johnson's *Dictionary of the English Language*. Most dictionaries are now informed by corpus studies, and many well-established names such as Oxford, Cambridge, Macmillan, and Merriam-Webster offer online versions of their dictionaries for free. Students can access these resources on their mobile devices as an alternative to purchasing expensive specialist electronic dictionaries, and as a way of engaging in more autonomous and proactive learning.

As well as traditional dictionaries, there is also a wide range of linguistic databases of different descriptions, offering everything from collocations to crowd-sourced example sentences to native speaker pronunciations to word "sketches" and much more. Some of these resources are suitable for self-access for higher-level learners, while others will require teacher curation and mediation, especially for lower-level learners.

Resources

Hardware

- Smartphone or tablet (iOS/Android)
- Desktop or laptop (Windows/Mac OS)

Software

- Hot Potatoes: Mac OS/Windows, http://hotpot.uvic.ca

Websites

- Merriam-Webster: http://learnersdictionary.com
- Cambridge Dictionary: https://dictionary.cambridge.org
- Oxford Learners' Dictionaries: http://www.oxfordlearnersdictionaries.com
- Macmillan Dictionary: http://www.macmillandictionary.com
- Simple Wiktionary: http://simple.wiktionary.org
- Tatoeba: http://www.tatoeba.org
- Read Lang: http://www.readlang.com
- Pop Jisyo: http://www.popjisyo.com
- Omega Wiki: http://www.omegawiki.org

- Sketch Engine for Language Learning (SkELL): https://skell.sketchengine.co.uk
- Forvo: https://forvo.com

————

30. Traditional lookup dictionaries: There are a number of traditional look-up style dictionaries available in digital form. One of the more innovative is the Simple Wiktionary, a community-created dictionary offering simplified definitions of English words specifically for non-native speakers of English.

————

31. Inline translation tools: A selection of online tools provide a means of overlaying words definitions as pop-ups or tool-tips, allowing word meanings to be checked without interrupting the flow of reading.

Read Lang and Pop-Jisyo both offer inline translation for a variety of language pairs, with Pop-Jisyo also allowing any website to be processed as a text. Read Lang offers teacher monitoring tools, which allow you to check, among other things, the most translated words within a class of students.

————

32. Word Sketches: The innovative Sketch Engine for

Language Learners (http://skell.sketchengine.co.uk), based on seminal work by the late and great computational linguist Adam Kilgariff, is a great way for learners to explore example sentences, similar words, and collocational "word sketches."

Word sketches show which words frequently surround the target word, and also provide part-of-speech information. This is a useful resource for helping learners to develop more naturalistic and idiomatic English usage.

CORPORA, WORD LISTS, AND LEXICAL PROFILING

Introduction

When Michael West produced his General Service List (GSL) of core English vocabulary in 1953, it was the culmination of 30 years of manual work (Carter & McCarthy, 1988). Computer readable corpora didn't come about until the 1960s, the first of which was the one-million-word Brown Corpus of Standard American English (Meyer, 2002).

Since that time, multi-billion-word corpora such as the Cambridge English Corpus have become the norm, and help us to ensure that the language we teach our students is "natural, relevant, and up to date" (Cambridge University Press, 2018).

Powerful concordancers and lexical profiling tools help us to understand how language is actually used, and allow us to analyze both native speaker and non-native speaker produced texts. Many of these tools are now available online through web interfaces, and offer a multitude of powerful features and functions.

Resources

Hardware

- Smartphone or tablet (iOS/Android)
- Desktop or laptop (Windows/Mac OS)

Websites

- Lex Tutor: http://www.lextutor.ca
- Text Inspector: http://www.englishprofile.org/wordlists/text-inspector
- Online Graded Text Editor: http://www.er-central.com/ogte
- WebCorp: http://www.webcorp.org.uk
- British National Corpus: http://www.natcorp.ox.ac.uk
- Corpus of Contemporary American English: http://corpus.byu.edu/coca
- iWeb Corpus: https://corpus.byu.edu/iweb
- Sentence Corpus of Remedial English: http://www.score-corpus.org/en/
- Michigan Corpus of Academic Spoken English: https://quod.lib.umich.edu/cgi/c/corpus/corpus
- Million Song Dataset:

https://labrosa.ee.columbia.edu/millionsong/musi
xmatch

- Open American National Corpus:
  http://www.anc.org

———

33. Lexical profiling: Lexical profiling—that is, analyzing the kind of language used in a text—can be used to help grade student-produced texts, or to judge whether a particular text is suitable for a certain level of student.

The Compleat Lexical Tutor lets teachers analyze any text using a variety of criteria. It includes several well-established word lists such as the Academic Word List (AWL), the General Service List (GSL), and the New General Service List (NGSL).

———

34. The Online Graded Text Editor: The Online Graded Text Editor (OGTE) is a lexical profiling tool for creating texts suitable for graded reading. Teachers and materials creators can easily check the percentage of on-list and off-list vocabulary in their text to ensure it is at the right level for students. OGTE provides three lists (General, GSL, and NGSL) divided into a range of frequency/difficulty levels.

———

35. Using online corpora: In addition to utilizing traditional grammar and lexis study activities, it's important to make students aware of more idiomatic English collocations. Corpora provide evidence of the most common and idiomatic English usage in written and spoken texts, and can be used as both language teaching and learning aids. Corpora such as the Corpus of Contemporary American English offer free web interfaces to their data.

One way to use corpora as a learning activity is to have students search for phrases they have used in their own written texts and look up how frequently the phrases appear in the corpora. The more frequently the phrase appears, the more idiomatic and natural sounding it is likely to be.

PART V

CLASSROOM MANAGEMENT

LEARNER MANAGEMENT SYSTEMS

Introduction

A Learner Management System (LMS) can help you to manage classes, record attendance and grades, distribute materials, and administer and evaluate reports, among other things.

Most educational institutions will already offer an LMS of some description, usually via one of the big players such as Moodle or Blackboard, which are installed on local networks.

There are also cloud-hosted solutions available, such as Edmodo or Schoology, which offer user-friendly LMS environments for teachers and their students.

Resources

Hardware

- Smartphone or tablet (iOS/Android)
- Desktop or laptop (Windows/Mac OS)

Software

- Moodle: http://www.moodle.org
- Blackboard: http://www.blackboard.com

Websites

- Edmodo: http://www.edmodo.com
- Schoology: https://www.schoology.com

———

36. Moodle: Moodle, which stands for Modular Object-Oriented Dynamic Learning Environment, was first released in 2001 and now has over 100,000 registered installations in 229 countries.

The main advantages of Moodle are its free and open source status, as well as the availability of numerous plugins to extend its functionality (http://moodle.org/plugins).

CLASSROOM RESPONSE SYSTEMS

Introduction

Classroom Response Systems (CRS) and Online Student Response Systems (OSRS) are computer systems and software designed to poll students and receive information, which can then be viewed and analyzed by the teacher in real time.

Initially rolled out as a separate hardware device, the best known of which is the iClicker, it is now cheaper and more convenient to use cloud-based OSRS, which allow students to respond via an app or web page on their own smartphones.

For classrooms where students do not have their own devices, paper-based response systems such as Plickers are also available.

The use of CRS and OSRS in second language classrooms has been shown to improve student participation and motivation (Mork, 2014) as well as allowing for increased interaction and providing the opportunity for self-assessment (Cardoso, 2010).

Resources

Hardware

- Smartphone or tablet (iOS/Android)
- Desktop or laptop (Windows/Mac OS)
- iClicker device: https://www.iclicker.com

Websites

- Socrative: http://www.socrative.com
- NearPod: http://www.nearpod.com
- Plickers: http://plickers.com
- Kahoot: https://kahoot.com
- Mentimeter: https://www.mentimeter.com
- Poll Everywhere: https://www.polleverywhere.com

—————

37. What would you do? Create a multiple-choice question using Socrative and send it to the students. Verbally pose a moral question with multiple-choice answers, such as

You find a wallet filled with money on the street. Do you:

1. Keep it for yourself
2. Hand it in to the police
3. Leave it where it is
4. Remove the money and throw away the wallet?

Ask students to respond honestly by selecting the corresponding letter. Results will be displayed in real time on the teacher's display, and can be projected on a screen for the whole class to see (nobody knows which students chose which answers). Students make a note of the class consensus. Repeat this process for further moral questions.

Once students get the gist of the game, ask them to write down their own moral questions, and come to the front of the class to pose them to their classmates.

As a final activity, have students write a summary of the class consensus for each question, say whether they agree with the consensus, and give reasons why or why not, e.g. *This class thinks that the death penalty should be abolished. I agree because....*

————

38. Kahoot!: Kahoot! is a great way to get students engaged in the learning process as a whole class. It's a gamified OSRS that allows teachers to create their own quizzes, as well as access a variety of pre-made ones on a wide variety of topics.

Quizzes support many different kinds of questions, including jumbled answers, discussions, and surveys. Users can add text, images, and videos to questions to make them more engaging and interactive.

When a quiz is complete, it can be shared with learners, who answer questions in real time on their mobile devices.

ADMINISTRATIVE TASKS

Introduction

One of the most powerful applications of technology in the classroom is making administrative tasks such as grading, planning, and attendance-taking less time-consuming and more convenient.

Although we should be careful to avoid using technology to enforce authoritarian classroom regimes (such as some of the more intrusive facial recognition systems used in Chinese schools), wise use of technology can certainly make us more efficient teachers, and allow us to access vital classroom records from a variety of devices in any time or place.

Resources

Hardware

- Smartphone or tablet (iOS/Android)
- Desktop or laptop (Windows/Mac OS)

Software

- Teacher Kit: iOS/Android/Windows,
  http://www.teacherkit.net
- Planbook: iOS/Mac OS/Windows,
  http://www.hellmansoft.com
- Teacher Aide Pro: Android,
  http://www.teacheraidepro.com

Websites:

- Class Dojo: http://www.classdojo.com

———

39. Grading and attendance with digital tools: There are
a multitude of specialist record-keeping apps available for
teachers on both mobile and desktop devices.

Teacher Kit (iOS/Android/Windows) is a fully
comprehensive solution that offers attendance, behavior,
and grading facilities, among others.

Another recommendation is PlanBook (iOS/Mac

OS/Windows), which is designed specifically for lesson planning.

————

40. Digitally incentivizing student behavior: Technology can be used to conveniently and effectively incentivize student behavior, beyond simply using apps to record instances of good and bad behavior.

Class Dojo offers an innovative and engaging way to give visual feedback to students on their behavior. An avatar is assigned to each student, and the teacher can then confer a negative or positive point on a case-by-case basis for desirable (e.g. *participating actively*) or undesirable (e.g. *arriving late*) behaviors.

Student accounts can also be created to allow students to track their own scores in detail, and customize their avatar.

PART VI

VOCABULARY AND GRAMMAR

GRAMMAR CORRECTION AND PLAGIARISM DETECTION

Introduction

Rudimentary grammar checkers have been around since the 1970s, with the launch of Writer's Workbench, which could detect punctuation and style inconsistencies. By the 1980s, the program could also detect "split infinitives, errors in spelling and punctuation, overly long sentences, wordy phrases, and passive sentences" (Macdonald et al, 1982).

In the 1990s, pattern matching was adopted to detect anomalies in grammar or style. For example, the pattern <subj-3rd-person> <verb-base-form> <object> would match the erroneous sentence "He play football" and flag an error accordingly (Liou, 1991). A rule-based pattern matching approach is still used in many modern grammar checkers, including the open-source Language Tool (www.languagetool.org).

Recent grammar checkers have adopted statistical approach to error spotting, whereby the rules to be applied are inferred from a tagged training corpus (Lin et al, 2011; Ehsan & Faili, 2013). Machine Learning and Natural Language Processing are also employed to make grammar checking more accurate and comprehensive.

Resources

Hardware

- Smartphone or tablet (iOS/Android)
- Desktop or laptop (Windows/Mac OS)

Websites

- Grammarly: http://www.grammarly.com
- Hemingway: http://www.hemingwayapp.com
- Turnitin: http://www.turnitin.com
- Paper Rater: http://www.paperrater.com
- English Grammar: https://www.englishgrammar.org
- Talk English: https://www.talkenglish.com/grammar
- Ginger Software: https://www.gingersoftware.com/grammarcheck
- Internet Grammar: http://www.ucl.ac.uk/internet-grammar
- Language Tool: https://languagetool.org
- Write and Improve: https://writeandimprove.com

––––––

41. Grammarly is one of the best-known grammar checking tools, with over 10 million daily active users (Lytvyn & Siu, 2018). It can detect spelling mistakes, grammar mistakes, punctuation errors, and misused words.

It also offers plagiarism detection and vocabulary suggestion functions for premium users.

––––––

42. Hemingway is a free web-app for improving the readability of texts by detecting excessively long sentences and other types of awkward styles.

However, remind your students not to blindly trust the corrections or suggestions of an automated grammar checker—rather, they should use those to call attention to areas that may have problems, and then should study those areas more closely.

VOCABULARY LEARNING

Introduction

As British linguist David Wilkins stated, "without grammar very little can be conveyed, without vocabulary nothing can be conveyed" (Wilkins, 1989). The importance of acquiring new vocabulary and bolstering one's knowledge of existing vocabulary is well accepted by second language teachers and learners.

Vocabulary experts such as Paul Nation maintain that students can acquire both implicit and explicit knowledge of new vocabulary by studying word cards, and can learn 50 words per week using such methods (Nation, 2011). Nation (2011) particularly recommends digital flashcard applications that can be used at any time and in any place.

There are many such digital flashcard tools available, including Quizlet, Memrise, and Anki. Another advantage of digital flashcards over traditional paper-based alternatives in the ease with which a Spaced Repetition System (SRS) of learning can be implemented, which helps to efficiently commit vocabulary to memory for longer periods of time (Ma, 2009).

Resources

Hardware

- Smartphone or tablet (iOS/Android)
- Desktop or laptop (Windows/Mac OS)

Websites

- Quizlet: http://www.quizlet.com
- Memrise: http://www.memrise.com
- Anki SRS: http://www.ankisrs.net
- Vocabulary.com: http://www.vocabulary.com

———

Tip 43. Creating digital sets of vocabulary: You can create your own custom sets of vocabulary for students to study using a variety of tools. Quizlet is one of the most well established flashcard tools available, and allows teachers and learners to create word sets containing text, images, and sound recordings.

Although not specifically made for English language learners, Quizlet offers millions of community-generated word sets for free, as well as a premium marketplace for professional quality content, such as corpus-derived TOEFL vocabulary (e.g. http://quizlet.com/apps4efl/folders).

———

Tip 44. Studying digital sets of vocabulary: Students can study word sets with tools such as Quizlet, Memrise, and Anki, and some of these tools also provide ways for teachers to monitor and track students' progress.

The major benefit of such systems is that they can be accessed on mobile devices and studied anywhere at any time, thus encouraging learners to be more proactive and independent beyond the walls of the language classroom.

EXTENSIVE READING

Introduction

Extensive reading (ER) is defined by the Extensive Reading Foundation (erfoundation.org) as "an approach to language learning that encourages students to read a large amount of books... that is relatively easy for them to understand."

Proponents of ER include the likes of Stephen Krashen (Mason & Krashen, 1997), Norbert Schmitt (Pigada & Schmitt, 2006), Paul Nation (Nation, 1997), Willy Renandya (2007), Rob Waring (Waring, 2012), and many other luminaries of language acquisition theory. Some would argue that if there were a magic bullet for second language learning, ER might just be it.

Vocabulary knowledge acquisition is the preeminent measurable effect of engaging in ER, but reading a lot of graded books for pleasure also stimulates gains in grammatical knowledge (Renandya, 2007), collocational knowledge (Webb et al, 2013), and spelling knowledge (Krashen, 1989).

As with all traditionally paper-based learning activities, ER has experienced a shift toward digital platforms in recent years, which is allowing students to read a greater range of titles in a more convenient way, while also providing a way for teachers to easily track and validate their students' reading for grading purposes.

Resources

Hardware

- Smartphone or tablet (iOS/Android)
- Desktop or laptop (Windows/Mac OS)

Websites

- Xreading: http://www.xreading.com
- ER Central: http://www.er-central.com

———

Tip 45. Xreading: Xreading provides a web-based library of professionally published graded readers, in addition to a comprehensive set of teacher tracking and monitoring tools. Audio is offered for the majority of the titles, and quizzes are also available to help teachers assess the amount of ER students have completed.

Tip 46. ER Central: ER Central offers hundreds of freely available graded texts and comprehension quizzes. Other innovative features include vocabulary learning activities, inline word definitions, and a variety of listening comprehension tasks.

ER Central also allows students to email their teachers progress reports, with more comprehensive student tracking facilities planned for the near future.

PART VII

SPEECH SYNTHESIS AND SPEECH RECOGNITION

SPEECH SYNTHESIS (TEXT-TO-SPEECH)

Introduction

The quality of computer-synthesized speech (TTS) has improved rapidly since the earliest attempts dating back to the 1970s. The technology has moved well beyond the robotic-sounding voice associated with the likes of Stephen Hawking. Highly intelligible and naturalistic speech synthesis is now generated by AI powered systems, including IBM's Watson and Google's DeepMind.

The use of TTS for language teaching and learning purposes has increased during the last decade, and several studies have shown its suitability and effectiveness (e.g. Gonzales, 2007; Handley, 2009; Pellegrini, Costa & Trancoso, 2012).

Resources

Hardware

- Smartphone or tablet (iOS/Android)
- Desktop or laptop (Windows/Mac OS)

Websites

- Voki: http://www.voki.com
- From Text to Speech:
  http://www.fromtexttospeech.com
- Amazon Polly: https://aws.amazon.com/polly
- Google Cloud text-to-speech:
  https://cloud.google.com/text-to-speech

―――――

Tip 47. Using text-to-speech (TTS) services: Modern text-to-speech (TTS) software can be used to automatically create very natural audio recordings of written text. Recent versions of Mac OS X (10.7+) have a text-to-speech facility built in. Users of iOS devices can easily listen to any text by highlighting it and selecting the "Speak" option from the contextual popup menu.

Several websites are available that also offer the functionality to convert text to speech.

Teachers can use TTS to create audio recordings for a variety of listening activities in class, or students can be taught how to use it in order to turn a reading practice into a listening practice, or to easily check the correct pronunciation for written texts.

AUTOMATIC SPEECH RECOGNITION (ASR)

Introduction

Automatic Speech Recognition (ASR) is the process by which computer systems and software recognize human speech. ASR is often incorporated into Computer Assisted Pronunciation Training (CAPT) tools in order to help language learners improve their pronunciation of target forms.

CAPT and ASR can be used to provide different kinds of automatic feedback on student speech, such as intelligibility (Gao, Srivastava & Salsman 2017) and approximation to native speaker norms (English Central, 2015). Both CAPT and ASR can help students to improve their fluency and pronunciation, as well as practice speaking when no human interlocutor is available.

The suitability of cloud-based ASR services (e.g. Siri and Google Speech) for language learning has been recently examined (Daniels & Iwago, 2017), and Google Speech was found particularly useful for administering online speaking tasks that allow for automated scoring and feedback. ASR is also used in automated speaking tests such as Pearson's Versant and ETS' TOEFL Practice Online.

It is becoming more common to semi or fully automate speech evaluation, and it may therefore be beneficial for students to practice speaking in a way that can be recognized and evaluated highly by ASR-based tests.

Resources

Hardware

- Smartphone or tablet (iOS/Android)
- Desktop or laptop (Windows/Mac OS) with mic

Software

- Google Chrome

Websites

- English Central: http://www.englishcentral.com
- Dictation.io: http://dictation.io

―――――

48. Sentence dictation: Provide a list of short sentences for students to say. Have students use an ASR facility (on a compatible smartphone or website) to recognize them pronouncing each sentence. You can award points for each word accurately recognized.

Remind students, however, that speech recognition is not one hundred percent accurate, even for native speakers. Some words, such as homophones and proper nouns, may not be correctly recognized.

———

49. Free dictation: Have students deliver a short monologue about a familiar topic, such as a self-introduction or a description of family members. Students use an ASR facility to recognize their speaking. They may need to pronounce punctuation marks ("period", "comma", "new line") for longer speeches, which will help draw their attention to English punctuation.

For classes in computer rooms, try using the speech recognition built into the latest versions of Google Chrome. A free interface for this functionality is provided at: https://dictation.io.

———

50. English Central: English Central is an innovative website where language learners can practice listening and speaking. The site allows users to watch videos on a variety of topics and then record themselves saying the same sentences as the speakers in the videos. Voice recognition technology is used to analyze the pronunciation of the learner's recorded utterances, and evaluate how closely they match the native speaker's pronunciation.

English Central offers some content for free, with additional content available after purchasing a paid subscription, which also allows teachers to track and monitor their students' progress.

BONUS TIP!

51. The author of this book curates and maintains a list of over 175 websites for English language teachers and learners located at: http://www.apps4efl.com/sites. Please check it out if you are interesting in further exploring web-based activities and tools.

REFERENCES

Akdeniz, N. O. (2017). Use of student-produced videos to develop oral skills in efl classrooms. International Journal on Language, Literature and Culture in Education, 4(1), 43–53.

Allan, M. (1985). *Teaching English with Video.* Essex: Longman.

Amazon. (2018). *What is Cloud Computing?* Retrieved from https://aws.amazon.com/what-is-cloud-computing/

Arshavskaya, E. (2018). The Routledge Handbook of Language Learning and Technology.

Biegel, K. (1998). It's show time: Video production in the EFL classroom. *The Language Teacher, 22*(8), 11-14.

Cambridge University Press. (2018). Cambridge English Corpus. Retrieved from http://www.cambridge.org/us/cambridgeenglish/better-learning/deeper-insights/linguistics-pedagogy/cambridge-english-corpus

Cardoso, W. (2010). Clickers in the ESL classroom: the students' perspective. *Contact, 36*(2), 36–55.

Carter, R., & McCarthy, M. (1988). *Vocabulary and language teaching*. New York: Longman.

Daniels, P., & Iwago, K. (2017) The suitability of cloud-based speech recognition engines for language learning. *JALT CALL Journal, 13*(3), 229-239.

Derla, K. (2016). More Than 90 Percent Of College Students Prefer Reading Paper Books Over E-Books. Tech Times. Retrieved from https://www.techtimes.com/articles/131055/20160205/more-than-90-percent-of-college-students-prefer-reading-paper-books-over-e-books.htm

East, M., & King, C. (2012). L2 learners' engagement with high stakes listening tests: does technology have a beneficial role to play? *CALICO Journal, 29*(2), 208.

Ehsan, N., & Faili, H. (2012). Grammatical and context-sensitive error correction using a statistical machine translation framework. *Software: Practice and Experience, 43*(2), 187–206. https://doi.org/10.1002/SPE.2110

English Central (2015). *EnglishCentral's Intellispeech[SM] Assessment System*. Retrieved from https://blog.englishcentral.com/2017/10/18/englishcentral-upgrades-its-intellispeech%E2%84%A0-speech-assessment-2/

Forrest, T. (1992). "Shooting your class: The videodrama approach to language acquisition." In S. Stempleski, & P. Arcario (Eds.), *Video in Second Language Teaching: Using, Selecting, and Producing Video for the Classroom.* TESOL Inc.

Gao, Y., Srivastava, B. M. L., & Salsman, J. (2017). *Spoken English Intelligibility Remediation with PocketSphinx Alignment and Feature Extraction Improves Substantially over the State of the Art.* Retrieved from https://arxiv.org/pdf/1709.01713.pdf

Gardner, W. (2016). *Digital textbooks are accompanied by caveats.* Japan Times. Retrieved from https://www.japantimes.co.jp/opinion/2016/04/29/comm entary/japan-commentary/digital-textbooks-accompanied-caveats

Goldstein, B. (2014). *A history of video in ELT.* Retrieved from https://www.teachingenglish.org.uk/article/ben-goldstein-a-history-video-elt

Gonzales, D. (2007). Text-to-Speech Applications Used in EFL Contexts to Enhance Pronunciation. *TESL-EJ, 11*(2).

Handley, Z. (2009). Is text-to-speech synthesis ready for use in computer-assisted language learning? *Speech Communication, 51*(10), 906-919.

Harmer, J. (2004). How to teach English: an introduction to the practice of English language teaching (13. impr). Harlow: Longman, Pearson Education.

Hedge, T. (2008). *Teaching and learning in the language classroom.* Oxford: Oxford University Press.

Hislope, K. (2009). Learning Language in a Virtual World. *International Journal of Learning, 15*(11), 51-58.

Katchen, J. E. (1991). *Video Cameras in EFL Classrooms: Utilizing the New Technology*. Presented at the Annual Meeting of the Chulalongkorn University Language Institute International Conference on Explorations and Innovations in English Teaching Methodology, Bangkok, 1991.

Kelty, J., Cooperman, A., & Lefferts, G. (1991). *Family Album USA*. New York: Maxwell Macmillan International.

Krashen, S. D., & Terrell, T. D. (1983). *The natural approach: Language acquisition in the classroom*. Pennsylvania State University: Phoenix ELT.

Krashen, S. (1989). We acquire vocabulary and spelling by reading: Additional evidence for the input hypothesis. *The Modern Language Journal, 73*(4), 440-464.

Lardinois, F. (2018). Duolingo hires its first chief marketing officer as active user numbers stagnate but revenue grows. Retrieved from https://techcrunch.com/2018/08/01/duolingo-hires-its-first-chief-marketing-officer-as-active-user-numbers-stagnate/

Lin, N. Y., Soe, K., & Thein, N. (2011). Chunk-based grammar checker for detection translated English sentences. *International Journal of Computer Applications, 28*(1), 7-12.

Liou, H. C. (1991). Development of an English grammar checker a progress report. *CALICO Journal*, *9*(1), 57-70.

Lytvyn, M. & Siu, E. (2018). GE 256: Max Lytvyn Reveals How He Grew Grammarly to 10M+ Active Daily Users without Funding (podcast). Retrieved from https://growtheverywhere.com/growth-everywhere-interview/grammarly-max-lytvyn/

Macdonald, N. H., Frase, L. T., Gingrich, P. S., & Keenan, S. A. (1982). The Writer's Workbench: Computer aids for text analysis. *Educational Psychologist*, *17*(3), 172-179.

Magid, L. (2012). *Google Drive: Hybrid of Cloud Storage and Cloud Computing*. Retrieved from https://www.huffingtonpost.com/larry-magid/google-drive-review_b_1471827.html

Mason, B., & Krashen, S. (1997). Extensive reading in English as a foreign language. *System*, *25*(1), 91-102.

McBride, K. (2009). Social-networking sites in foreign language classes: Opportunities for re-creation. *The next generation: Social networking and online collaboration in foreign language learning*, *8*, 35-58.

Meyer, C. F. (2002). *English corpus linguistics: An introduction*. Cambridge University Press.

Mork, C. M. (2014). Benefits of using online student response systems in Japanese EFL classrooms. *JALT CALL Journal*, *10*(2), 127-137.

Nagaraj, G. (2003). *English Language Teaching: Approaches, Methods, Techniques*. Orient Longman.

Nation, I. S. P. (2011). My ideal vocabulary teaching course. In J. Macalister & I. S. P. Nation (Eds), Case studies in language curriculum design: concepts and approaches in action around the world (pp. 49-62). Routledge.

Nation, P. (1997). The language learning benefits of extensive reading. *The Language Teacher, 21*(5). Retrieved from https://jalt-publications.org/tlt/articles/2134-language-learning-benefits-extensive-reading

Nunan, D. (1997). Listening in language learning. *The Language Teacher, 23*(9), 47-51.

O'Mara. (2016). How Much Paper is Used in One Day? Retrieved from https://www.recordnations.com/2016/02/how-much-paper-is-used-in-one-day/

O'Reilly, T. (2009). *What is Web 2.0?*. O'Reilly Media.

Pigada, M., & Schmitt, N. (2006). Vocabulary acquisition from extensive reading: A case study. *Reading in a Foreign Language, 18*(1), 1-28.

Pellegrini, T., Costa, A., & Trancoso, I. (2012). Less errors with TTS? A dictation experiment with foreign language learners. *INTERSPEECH-2012*, 1291-1294.

Richards, J. C., & Renandya, W. A. (Eds.). (2013). *Methodology in language teaching: an anthology of current practice* (1st publ., 17. print). Cambridge: Cambridge Univ. Press.

Saville-Troike, M. (2006). *Introducing second language acquisition*. Cambridge, UK; New York: Cambridge University Press.

Schwartz, M. (1995). Computers and the language laboratory: learning from history. *Foreign Language Annals, 28*(4), 527–535.

Singer, N. (2017). *How Google Took Over the Classroom*. Retrieved from https://www.nytimes.com/2017/05/13/technology/google-education-chromebooks-schools.html

Stempleski, S. (1992). "Teaching communication skills with authentic video". In S. Stempleski, & P. Arcario (Eds.), *Video in Second Language Teaching: Using, Selecting, and Producing Video for the Classroom*. TESOL Inc.

Vesselinov, R., & Grego, J. (2012). *Duolingo effectiveness study*. City University of New York, USA. Retrieved from http://static.duolingo.com/s3/DuolingoReport_Final.pdf

Wang, S., & Camilla, V. (2012). Web 2.0 and second language learning: What does the research tell us?. *Calico Journal, 29*(3), 412.

Waring, R. (2012). *The inescapable case for extensive reading*. Retrieved from http://www.robwaring.org/er/what_and_why/er_is_vital.htm

Webb, S., Newton, J., & Chang, A. (2013). Incidental learning of collocation. *Language Learning, 63*(1), 91-120.

Wilkins, D. A. (1989). *Linguistics in language teaching*.
London: Arnold.

Zheng, D., Young, M. F., Wagner, M. M. & Brewer, R. A.
(2009). Negotiation for Action: English Language Learning
in Game–Based Virtual Worlds. *The Modern Language Journal*,
93, 489-511.